DOG ACT

A POST-APOCALYPTIC COMEDY BY
Liz Duffy Adams

The Rules in Brief

1) Do NOT perform this Play without obtaining prior permission from Playscripts, and without paying the required royalty.

2) Do NOT photocopy, scan, or otherwise duplicate any part of this book.

3) Do NOT alter the text of the Play, change a character's gender, delete any dialogue, or alter any objectionable language, unless explicitly authorized by Playscripts.

4) DO provide the required credit to the author and the required attribution to Playscripts in all programs and promotional literature associated with any performance of this Play.

For more details on these and other rules, see the opposite page.

Copyright Basics

Playscripts, Inc.
450 Seventh Ave, Suite 809
New York, NY 10123

toll-free phone: 1-866-NEW-PLAY
email: info@playscripts.com
website: www.playscripts.com

Dedicated to my tribe, New Dramatists

Cast of Characters

ROZETTA STONE (ZETTA), a woman. Performer and entrepreneur, from a long lineage of show-folk; inheritor of the Cart. Younger than Vera, probably a bit older than Dog.

DOG, a young male. Human by birth, dog by choice. His dog behavior is minimal and subtle. When he barks, as indicated, he does not make barking sounds; he shouts the word "bark."

VERA SIMILITUDE, gray-haired woman.

JO-JO THE BALD-FACED LIAR, a semi-feral teenaged girl. May wear a battered old etch-a-sketch on a bit of rope, for self-medication.

COKE & BUD, scavengers: savage grown-up Lost Boys, underfed and vicious, late-teens to 20s. They're dressed in odds and ends of found clothes and objects, including some bits of light armor hand-made from salvaged junk; incorporated into one of these is an ancient flattened-out Coke can; into the other, a Bud can. Coke is dominant, Bud aspirational.

Casting Note

The cast should be ethnically and racially mixed. The suggestion through casting that the various tribes are racially defined should be rigorously avoided.

.

Time & Place

Later on. A wilderness in the Northeast of the former USA.

Act 1: Night. A clearing.

Act 2: Late afternoon into night. On the edge of some ruins.

Notes on Playing Style

A paragraph break within one character's lines indicates a transition; not necessarily a pause but a shift. Words such as "har" or "heh" are meant to be treated as words, not laughs or breaths. The style is not overly naturalistic, but what you might call both theatrical and truly felt. The recommended model is Shakespearian: acting on the words.

Notes on Set / Props

A single set, mostly bare. The major set element is Zetta's cart. It is large enough for the characters to enter, with wheels, a fold-out stage, painted drops and posters, storage, hanging lanterns, poles to pull by and/or a harness. It must be light and nimble enough for the actors to move around the stage, and it must be transformable into a stage itself. It may be cobbled together from partly recognizable objects originally of other uses. It is old, travel-stained and weather-battered, and bursting with costumes, props, musical instruments, cooking utensils, books, and flotsam and jetsam of past ages, such as but not necessarily — just to give you the idea — broken clocks, a Russian Orthodox icon, a laughing Buddha, a Menorah, an Agent Mulder Action Figure, a tattered Keith Haring barking dog umbrella, a Star Trek lunch box, a banged-up computer monitor with the glass removed to serve as a puppet stage, puppets made from plastic flamingos, a Gumby, voodoo dolls, and botanica saints; things with unknown purposes made of spare parts from obsolete objects like toaster ovens, doorknobs, telephones, CDs, a Statue of Liberty pencil sharpener, and so on.

The musical instruments are handmade from various found objects, and function practically like guitars, horns, xylophones, percussive instruments, etc. while being clearly unique and make-shift. All the music is meant to be created on stage by the actors.

The weapons, similarly, are salvaged, low-tech variations on bow-and-arrows, spears, knives and so on. Perhaps a rifle has been turned into a cross-bow, or a pistol serves as the handle for a long dagger.

Acknowledgments

Dog Act was originally produced by The Shotgun Players (Patrick Dooley, Artistic Director; Liz Lisle, Managing Director) in collaboration with Playwrights Foundation (Amy Mueller, Artistic Director) at The Thick House in San Francisco in September, 2004, moving to The Ashby Stage in Berkeley, California. It was directed by Kent Nicholson with set design by Praba Pilar and Stewart Port, lighting design by Rob Anderson and costume design by Valera Coble. The original cast was as follows:

ROZETTA STONE.................... Beth Donohue
DOG .... Richard Bolster
VERA SIMILITUDE ....Dianne Manning
JO-JO THE BALD-FACED LIAR.........Rami Margron
COKE..................................Eric Burns
BUD..................................Dave Maier

Dog Act was developed at the Bay Area Playwrights Foundation and Portland Stage Company's Little Festival of the Unexpected. It was awarded the 2004 Will Glickman Playwright Award for the Best New Play in the Bay Area.

Special thanks to David Rhodes for musical notation.

Sylvia M'Lafi Thompson and Jo Anne Glover in *Dog Act*, MOXIE
Theatre, San Diego (2005). Photo: Tim Bradstreet.

DOG ACT

A PLAY WITH MUSIC

by Liz Duffy Adams

ACT I

(Autumn. Night. Wilderness. ZETTA enters cautiously.)

ZETTA. *(Stage whisper:)* Dog. Dog. Where you, Dog?

> *(She whistles low. Noises off, screams and yells. ZETTA hides in the shadows. COKE and BUD enter with a large, heavily filled sack.)*

COKE. Fuck this fucker, fuck-all heavy.

BUD. Fuck yeah. And will not cease to struggle, thou fuck. *(Strikes sack.)*

COKE. Yoi! Do not thou fuck with my prize, I want it lively for the sacrifice.

BUD. Thy prize?

COKE. Fuck yeah, mine. I saw it, I fucking caught it, I will fucking eat its fucking brains at fucking midnight and the gillies will all fucking compete to fuck me, yeah.

BUD. The fuck you say.

COKE. The fuck I do say.

BUD. Thou fuck-lobe, I saw it first.

COKE. Fuck thy freeze-dried scrotum, it's mine.

BUD. In a mutant's anus, thou quark-witted son of a three-eyed stump-licker.

COKE. So's yer mother.

BUD. FUCK.

(They drop the sack and begin attempting to throttle each other. JO-JO crawls out of the sack, snatches up another bag and scrambles off. After a moment, COKE breaks away and sees what's happened.)

COKE. Yoi! It scramoosed!

BUD. With our caboodle to boot, the god-fucking whore of a god-fucked fucker!

COKE. Let slip the hound-droogs, ah-oooh!

BUD. Ah-oooh!

(Howling, they turn to pursue—and discover ZETTA. A very tense pause. Then ZETTA performs a little dance, ending with a flourishing bow. The Scavengers exchange disgusted looks.)

COKE. It's a fucking vaudevillian.

BUD. Fuck that.

(They resume their howling pursuit and exit. As the sound of them dies down ZETTA whistles cautiously again for DOG.)

ZETTA. *(Low:)* Here, boy. Here, boy. Damn you, Dog, come the hell on.

(DOG enters behind her.)

DOG. Hey.

ZETTA. *(Jumps.)* DAMN. Dog. Where you been?

DOG. Sniffing around.

ZETTA. Anything?

DOG. Bad place.

ZETTA. No joke, puppy. Scavengers on the roam and where you? "Sniffing around." Come when called next time, damn the bitch what bore you, hey?

DOG. Okay, Zetta. Where's the cart?

ZETTA. Safe, safe, no fear. Hid her back over there. Wait. What you smell?

DOG. All clear. Hunt moved on southward.

ZETTA. Okay. Good Dog. Go on.

> (DOG *goes off.* ZETTA *looks around, listening for the Scavengers.*)

Southward, hey. Well, he got a good nose.

> (DOG *enters pulling the cart.* ZETTA *lights a lantern and they take what they need to get comfortable, while:*)

I tell you what, Dog, this do suck. This do suck like a succubus suck.

DOG. At least we still have the cart.

ZETTA. So the god-fugged what? We got cart, we got costume, we got strum-strings and jing-jang-whackers and we got fug-all if we got no bodies to go with! Ever since Smack and Jelly got eaten up in Kinarsey and the freaks defected to the N'orlin Freak Kingdom we been down to the bare wish-bone.

DOG. Got me.

ZETTA. A dog act. One one-dog dog act. One one-trick one-dog dog act. Listen oh listen, I have seen and been better days and ways. I have seen and been. How we going to perform for the King of China when we get there? No mortality play, no orchestramie, no dancing gillies, no freaks not even.

DOG. Nada mucho.

ZETTA. You have said it.

DOG. Rub my head.

ZETTA. *(Doing so:)* What will the King of China say when he sees solemente us, bare-ragged, foot-fagged, lacking all but the least of entertainment necessities?

DOG. What indeed?

ZETTA. He be sans speech. He be disappointed down to his DNA and have no not a word to exsanguinate his soul-sadness forth, by with.

DOG. DNA?

ZETTA. Damn Near All. He be heart-busted.

DOG. Anyway, any luck we won't get there.

ZETTA. Won't need any luck for that. Just the self-same brand of anti-luck we be running with.

(DOG *begins to play one of their make-shift instruments.*)

Hey, now, Dog, we got to keep it on the quiet.

DOG. It's safe, Zetta. Trust me.

(DOG *sings the first line of the song:*)

DON'T ASK ME WHY

(*Pause. He starts again:*)

DON'T ASK ME WHY

ZETTA. (*Singing:*) DON'T ASK ME WHAT

ZETTA & DOG. (*Singing together:*)
DON'T ASK ME NOTHIN' NOTHIN' NOTHIN' NOTHIN' BUT
HOO HOO, HOO HAH
WE'RE WALKIN'
JUST WALKIN'
WALKIN' TO CHI-I-NA

THE KING OF CHINA
HE SENT TO ME
A MESSENGER OF SUCH IMMENSE CIVILITY
HOO HOO, HOO HEY
JUST WALKIN'
YEAH WALKIN'
WALKIN' TO CHI-I-NA

NO ONE KNOW WHERE
THAT CHINA BE
WE ONLY KNOW IT WHERE THE SUN COME OUT THE SEA
HOO HOO, HOO HOH
WE'RE WALKIN'
JUST WALKIN'
WALKIN' TO CHI-I-NA

SAID DOG AND ZETTA!
NOBODY BETTER!
WALKIN' TO CHI-I-NAAAA!

> *(Above, they may sometimes alternate lines playfully; overall, it's
> a song that cheers them up. On the final note of their big finish, the
> earth wobbles violently, signaled by a sound-effect like booming
> thunder.)*

ZETTA & DOG. WOOOOOOH!

> *(They start to lose gravity, then the earth resumes its normal spin
> and they stagger and fall down. It is abruptly much colder. Maybe
> even some flakes of snow.)*

ZETTA. Damn-all, winter again? Winter last week.

DOG. *(Shivering:)* Frrrrrrrrr.

> (ZETTA *pulls out warm costume pieces, clothing or blankets.)*

ZETTA. Here, Dog, bundle. *(Stamps on the ground.)* Settle out and fly
straight why dontcha?

DOG. I hate when it does that. *(Sneezing:)* Ach-ooo!

ZETTA. Okay, there, Dog, get under there.

> *(They huddle together for warmth, maybe under the remnant of a
> velvet stage curtain.)*

Damn thing got the wobbly shakes and we got to shake along with.
Time we get to the sea it be all spilt out, this rate.

DOG. Tell me something, Zetta.

ZETTA. Tell you what?

DOG. Tell me about the sea.

ZETTA. I told you.

DOG. Tell me again.

ZETTA. The sea… It the Big Wet. It the prime-odial stuff of all stuff. It got the roar of a monster and the harsh of a whisper. It thicker than blood and fiercer than weather. It draw you to it, and then it drag you in and make you drink, and when you drink you want to stay, and never breath no rank old air again. Then it got you, and you stay got. It deep and cold and fat and wild and I will know it when I see it.

DOG. When will we see it?

ZETTA. Maybe in the spring.

DOG. Maybe tomorrow.

ZETTA. We smell it first. The sea may be smelt from afar.

DOG. What's it smell like?

ZETTA. It smell like a come-on meeting a want-to. Like a knife's edge meeting a peach, metallic hoo-hah and salt.

DOG. It's been a long time since I've had salt. Or a peach.

ZETTA. I never had neither. Where you have salt, Dog? Dog?

DOG. We have any of that food left?

ZETTA. What, that squirrel?

DOG. Wasn't a squirrel.

ZETTA. Don't start. What was if not squirrel?

DOG. No squirrel ever had scales and gills.

ZETTA. Well, ain't no fish ever got a fluffy tail and run up a tree. Call it a squish if you want to, we ate the last of it yesterday.

DOG. Squish. Flurrel. Flurrel is better.

ZETTA. Flurrel. Write it down, why not.

DOG. We haven't seen any others, no point in noting anomalies.

Anyhow. Dogs don't write.

ZETTA. A-nom-u-lee. I bet you can write, Dog.

DOG. Not anymore.

ZETTA. But I bet you can—

DOG. Grrrrr…

ZETTA. *(Sharply:)* Dog!

> *(She watches him sternly until he stops growling and hangs his head penitently. Then she lets it go.)*

We go hunting first-light, catch something to eat. Fug-hat, soon's the sky's clear and we get some star light we start out walking, hey? Faster we get outa this the better. Scavengers got no proper appreciation of culture. Get someplace a little bit organized, hey? Got to be a tribal boundary around here somewhere, find us a town some kind, put up your act and a song. Maybe somebody be ready to bust out of tribe, come on the road, train 'em up for the play, hey? Damn-all, wish it ain't winter again.

DOG. Never know, might be spring any minute.

ZETTA. Any minute or never what-all. Spring mighta got lost in the trans-nation, caught in the gears o' time, never to be seen, felt nor smelt again. Might could stick on winter for good and all, till our froz-ed toes snap like twigs and when we get to the sea he froze too.

DOG. Like to see that.

ZETTA. Hell you would.

DOG. Spring'll come, Zetta.

ZETTA. You cheering me up, snoopy?

DOG. Don't know. Am I?

ZETTA. Shut it, Dog.

> *(Slight pause.)*

DOG. Tell me about China.

ZETTA. I don't know. I don't know what-all about China.

DOG. You do. You know all, Zetta.

ZETTA. That so?

DOG. You know you know all, Zetta. You could add it to the bill. Ask The Amazing All-Knowing Zetta, No Question Unanswered.

ZETTA. I do. I do know all. Know why?

DOG. Because you are unfettered by any fanatical reverence for facts.

I mean. I mean. Why, Zetta?

ZETTA. I know all. Because. I got the cart. And with the cart come ancient wisdom and knowledge and know-how and the sacred-freaking-flame of the olden days and ways and the lore of the golden age, the silver age, the brassy age and the age of plastic, you follow me, puppy?

DOG. Sure, Zetta.

Say, Zetta, what's this China I've heard you speak of?

ZETTA. Say, Dog, glad you asked. Who-all has not heard of that wonder-ous city, and yet who-all has seen it with they own eyes and can so say? Far and so-so-far-'n-fablisimo: Chi-na; even the name a very chime of phantas-no-goria. Across a vasty-wide plain-old plain, a many-days slog of dry empty nada-mucho, no food, no drink, no rest from weary nor longing nor gathering gut-gloominess of bur-dened spirit and foot-drag. Only just when hope be not just lost but found again then tramped down spat on beat all to fug-hat and back, only then: a glimmer is seen on the edge of far-off. Is it? Oh my sacred and profane golly yes. A glimmer comes a gleam, a gleam a glitter as nearer we come. Then you in China, and it like nothing you ever thought you might of maybe one time dreamed. Every step bring a eye-goggling wonder. There a pointy tower so high when you climb up there you can see tomorrow. There a stone woman higher even nor that, hollow inside with stairs, and from the top you look out her eyes and see day after tomorrow. All around, buildings tall, old and old, gold stone higher than you can see, shimmer-shammyin' in the tender old sun. But the most important thing about China of all and all? The people. And the most important thing about the people: they wise. They so wise. They know the past, they imagine the future. And this because in the very center of China, there a very particular building. Stone. Old stone. Big around as would take half a day to walk. Door guarded by two vasty-big beasts, monster-osities of the old times, last of their kind. You want to enter, got to get past them, and if you want to get past them, you got to answer their question. No one know what that question be; it can't be remembered what-all. Get it right, you in with a fin. And then you really someplace. That building be filled with everything ever forgotten, everything ever known, everything can be known. Filled with fine, fine, moo-ie fine info-mation, yeah. It be the reservoir. It be bliss. But. You can't answer the question? Beasts devour you on the spot. Critter on the left take off your head in one clean bite. Critter on the right swallow your body. Snap, crunch, gulp, gone.

And that be what-all I know about China.

How 'bout you, Dog?

DOG. What?

ZETTA. What do you know?

DOG. About China?

ZETTA. About anything what-all.

DOG. I don't know anything. Dogs don't know anything, Zetta.

ZETTA. Dog, I tell you history, I tell you songs, I tell you stories, I tell all the info-mation I got and you take it. But you don't tell nothing back.

DOG. I pull my weight.

ZETTA. Nobody say you don't. You a good dog.

DOG. That's right.

ZETTA. I just want to know, * Dog —

DOG. (*Overlapping:*) Leave it alone, * Zetta —

ZETTA. (*Overlapping:*) WHY you a dog, Dog, and what * you know —

DOG. (*Overlapping:*) Leave it alone, Zetta, or I'll be one of those dogs that don't even talk.

> (*Slight pause.*)

ZETTA. (*Brusquely:*) Stars'r out. Let's walk.

> (*They start putting stuff away. DOG begins whistling or humming, or plucking an instrument, but ZETTA ignores him. Then DOG sings the first two lines, and ZETTA joins in finally with the third. They alternate the rhyming lines and come in together on the repeating lines — a "rhyme this" game.*)

DOG. THE WANG-TAILED WALLOW CAUGHT THE 32-SNUP
SAY HEY AND A HEY TILL YOU BUST A STANGLE

ZETTA. AND IT MADE IT ALL THE WAY TO THE ANTE-UP

ZETTA & DOG. HO, HO, THE WRANGLE.

ZETTA. THE WALLOW AND THE JU-JEE CAUGHT THE 84-S-NAP

ZETTA & DOG. SAY HEY AND A HEY TILL YOU BUST A STANGLE

DOG. THEN THE GAZABO COPPED IT UP THE HINKY-HAP

ZETTA & DOG. HO, HO, THE WRANGLE.

DOG. THE JUJEE PULLED A WOOLLY ON THE 22-SNOUT

ZETTA & DOG. SAY HEY AND A HEY TILL YOU BUST A STANGLE

ZETTA. SO THE WALLOW HOLLERED SAMMY TILL THEY CHEESED IT OUT

ZETTA & DOG. HO, HO, THE WRANGLE.

ZETTA. THE LIMP-A-LONE SNOOKER SNAGGED THE JUJEE'S LAST BAP

ZETTA & DOG. SAY HEY AND A HEY TILL YOU BUST A STANGLE

DOG. BUT THE BULLS BIFFED COKEY SO THEY TIPPED THE TAP

ZETTA & DOG. HO, HO, THE WRANGLE.

> *(Maybe they end with a flourish, or maybe* DOG's *about to start a new verse. But he senses someone offstage and rushes off barking, while* ZETTA *snatches up a weapon.)*

DOG. BARK! BARK, BARK! BARK!

> *(VERA and* JO-JO *run in, herded by* DOG, *stopping when they see* ZETTA *holding the weapon on them.* VERA *holds her hands out, palms up, and nudges* JO-JO *to do the same.)*

ZETTA. Okay, Dog. Good boy.

DOG. Grrrr.

JO-JO. Told you, Vere, a man.

ZETTA. Keep your hands out. And he a dog.

JO-JO. Oh. Sure?

ZETTA. *(To* VERA:*)* What you be? What tribe?

VERA. None.

ZETTA. *(To* VERA:*)* I asked you.

JO-JO. No tribe. Believe it. She don't lie. She a Vera.

VERA. Vera Similitude. At your service. Only truth told.

ZETTA. Yeah? Tell the future?

JO-JO. Future? Har. She do better an that. She tell the present.

VERA. My young associate and I intend no harm. We are vaudevillians, like yourselves, or so I surmise from your apparatus.

ZETTA. Gear on the ground. Go on.

> (*They place everything they carry on the ground.*)

Check 'em out, Dog.

> (DOG *starts to frisk and sniff them and their belongings carefully.*)

ZETTA. So. You roadsters? Where your company?

JO-JO. Long story. Don' ask don' smell.

ZETTA. Asking you, Vera.

VERA. We were down to only five of us. The others men. We found ourselves in a perilous predicament, having wandered unwittingly deep within the tribal borders of a militaristic matriarchal free-market slave-economy. They were profoundly interested in the breeding potential of our compatriots and ultimately we found it irresistibly advantageous to part with them.

ZETTA. You sold 'em?

VERA. One might perhaps more precisely express it as a irrefusable reward for accepting gracefully an unavoidable event and eschewing the shedding of blood which would undoubtedly in the circumstances have been our own.

ZETTA. That what truth sound like?

VERA. Ah. You may have absolute confidence in the meaning of my content, but you must forgive me my elaborations of form, my dear. When only truth may be told, obfuscation of style is very strongly advised.

ZETTA. Huh. What happen to your cart? And what you * doing round here—

JO-JO. (**Interrupting:*) HEY FUCK THIS ASKIN' ASKIN' KEEP YER DOG OFF I CUT HE SNIFFIN * NOSE—

VERA. *(*Overlapping:)* Now, now, now…

ZETTA. *(At the same time:)* Come 'ere, boy.

> *(JO-JO sits or turns away and calms herself with her battered old etch-a-sketch.)*

What her deal?

VERA. Allow me to present Jo-Jo, The Bald-Faced Liar. Stories told, ancient and marvelous, no veracity guaranteed.

ZETTA. Story-teller?

VERA. She holds them verbatim in her teeming brain, however unlikely her demeanor may strike you, and she can recite same, for proper remuneration.

ZETTA. Huh. Soothsayer and story-teller. What else you got?

VERA. Perhaps, before we satisfy more of your no doubt justifiable curiosity, it would be well to establish new parameters for our group dynamic. We saw your cart and supposed you might be moved to view us in the light of tribal kinship, and offer us succor, if not a merging of the ways. May we not establish at least a temporary peace?

> *(ZETTA considers this, then puts her weapon down. DOG and JO-JO tense. She takes a step toward VERA, who takes a step toward her. They both ritualistically display "nothing up my sleeves," then bow, maintaining eye-contact until the last moment, lowering their heads for a bare instant then snapping them both up warily. This trust rite completed, they step back.)*

VERA. May I receive it then, that my assumption was correct? You are of the trade?

ZETTA. I am Zetta Stone, and THIS *(She pulls a rope on the front of the cart and a painted banner appears:)* is ROZETTA STONE'S POST-'POC SNAKE-CIRCLING TRAVELING VAUDEVILLE & FREAK SHOW, SONG AN DANCE EXTRAV-NO-GANZA WITH DOG-ACT AN MORTALITY PLAY CURRENTLY UNDER CONTRACTUAL OBLIGATION TO THE KING OF CHINA, SECOND TO NO-ONE AND NO MONEY BACK.

VERA. I am extraordinarily gratified to make your acquaintance.

ZETTA. This Dog. He don't bite.

> *(A moment between* DOG *and* VERA, *a look. Perhaps she offers her hand for him to sniff.)*

VERA. Dog.

DOG. Madame Similitude.

VERA. Jo-Jo. These are now friends. A greeting.

JO-JO. Yeah. Just: dog or no dog, he lay a paw on me he pay, one way or other.

DOG. Trust me.

ZETTA. Okay then.

> *(They sit down, still in wary, separate pairs, as if to a parlay.)*

Let's see what you got. How this truth-telling work? You answer any question?

VERA. Assuredly.

ZETTA. Why the earth wobble?

VERA. I don't know.

ZETTA. What's the meaning of life?

VERA. I have no idea.

ZETTA. How the stars stay up?

VERA. Not a clue, my dear.

> *(Slight pause.)*

ZETTA. Not much of an act.

VERA. Sadly, that is also true.

ZETTA. How 'bout a story from your little short-fuse there?

(Almost before ZETTA *finishes speaking,* JO-JO *launches abruptly and ferociously into her story. She speaks relentlessly without pauses and without comment, the story having been memorized word-for-word; she uses no story-telling arts.)*

JO-JO. "ONCE IN THE LONG AGO TIME Fox went looking for a wife, he was poor, he had only one horse because he was lazy so he went looking for a rich wife, he heard of a woman, the daughter of a chief that no one wanted because she was a witch, he went to that village on the plains where they live in clay houses, he sat with the chief, they smoked together, he said I will marry your daughter but you must give me one hundred horses, the chief agreed, the daughter was sent for, Fox was pleased, she was beautiful and he had one hundred horses, the next day they set out to return to Fox's home, when a little time had passed he thought to count his horses, there were only ninety but ten ducks were flying back the way they had come, after more time had passed he stopped to count again, there were only seventy horses but twenty snakes were wriggling back the way they had come, some time later he counted again, what do you think? only forty horses and thirty hornets buzzing back the way they had come, by the time they reached Fox's home he had only the horse he had started with and his new wife, he was angry and raised his knife to kill her, she became an eagle and flew up but he threw his knife and hit her in the wing, she fell back, she became a woman again, he put her in a dark pit without food, he told her you are a witch but you will be my witch and help me avenge myself on your father for tricking me, every day she grew weaker, one day he let her back into the light and he pointed at the sun: see how bright the moon is tonight? she said that is the sun, he put her back in the pit, another night he let her out again and he pointed at the moon: isn't the sun hot today? she said that is the moon, back in the pit, the next time he let her out he said do you see the moon? she said yes there is the moon, he said are you blind? that is the sun, she said forgive me, it is the sun, it is whatever you say it is, then Fox knew she was his witch, he gave her some food and they set off toward her father's village, as soon as she had eaten she grew stronger, as soon as she grew stronger she turned into a wolf and she killed Fox SHE WAS NOT HIS WITCH HE HAD BEEN WRONG ABOUT THAT."

(JO-JO bows abruptly and sits again.)

ZETTA. Not bad, what-all. Socko finish.

DOG. What's it mean?

JO-JO. Huh?

DOG. What's the story mean, what's it about, what do the man and woman represent, what is witch a metaphor for, is the sun/moon dichotomy significant in gender terms, what's it mean?

    (Slight pause. JO-JO *stands up again.)*

JO-JO. "ONCE IN THE LONG-AGO TIME, Fox went looking for a wife, * he was poor —"

VERA. *(* Overlapping:)* That will do, my dear, never mind.

ZETTA. *(To* DOG, *sharply:)* What-all with you?

DOG. Sorry, sorry, never mind, I'm sorry.

ZETTA. What else you got?

VERA. For select and sophisticated audiences of mature age we offer a special curiosity for an additional fee: "The Tableau of Human Tenderness."

    (VERA and JO-JO *form a tableau, a tender embrace. There is nothing salacious about it. They hold for a moment, then bow.)*

ZETTA. Huh. We could use that. Set up a peep show behind the cart, hey, Dog?

DOG. I guess.

VERA. Also: singing, dancing and pretending to feel things, of course.

ZETTA. What do ya sing?

VERA. We have an extensive repertoire of standards. Do you know "Weed World?"

    (She hums a bar, and DOG *— or another of them — begins to play accompaniment.)*

VERA. *(Singing:)*
I'M JUST A WEEDY GIRL
IN THIS WEEDY SEEDY WORLD
WITH NOT MUCH LEFT TO DO

BUT SURVEY THE GLOOMY VIEW
OF THE END OF WHAT WE KNEW
SO I'D LIKE TO SAY TO YOU…

IN THIS AGE OF SLOW DECLINE
DON'T YOU DECLINE TO BE MINE
IN THIS ERA OF DECAY
WON'T YOU SAY WITH ME YOU'LL STAY

AND AS A WEEDY GIRL AND BOY
WHAT'S LEFT OF WEED WORLD WE'LL ENJOY
FOR I WOULD GLADLY BE EXTINCT
IF MY EPITAPH WHEN INKED
READ: SHE WENT THE WAY OF DINO
BUT SHE LOVED A BOY DIVINE-OH!

> *(An instrumental break,* VERA *dances a soft-shoe, then continues the song.)*

YES… I… AM…JUST A WEEDY GIRL
IN THIS SEEDY WEEDY WORLD
BUT IF YOU SAY YOU LOVE ME TRUE
I'LL GLADLY CLING TO LIFE WITH YOU
TILL COCKROACHES AND ZEBRA MUSSELS
ARE ALL THAT'S LEFT FOR US TO STEW
I WON'T BOO-HOO…
IF I HAVE YOU…
IN WEED…WEED…WORLD

ZETTA. Class act. Moo-ie jiggie.

VERA. And when the market is propitious Jo-Jo rents out her body for sexual purposes.

ZETTA. She keep that or pool it?

VERA. Oh, pool, assuredly, after a top-share. Jo-Jo is a team-player.

That is, in a sense, and taking into account, and so on.

JO-JO. Choose my own tricks.

ZETTA. Yeah, sure. And you-all know the mortality play, got your parts down stone?

VERA. Naturally.

ZETTA. Well, there, now, Vera, don't mind saying it: you a true vaudster, and welcome to walk along with. Shake-down tour, any-how, see how we fit. Sound okay?

VERA. Indubitably, a most welcome invitation.

ZETTA. Okay, then, no blinding contract, but we a patch-company for now and for sure. Come on, critters, company-greet.

> *(They perform a brief, ritual version of theatrical greeting: first ZETTA with VERA, a highly-stylized double air-kiss. DOG and JO-JO do the same, reluctantly.)*

ZETTA & VERA. *(Deadpan:)* Darling.

DOG & JO-JO. *(Mumbling/growling, reluctant:)* Darling.

ZETTA. *(To cap the ritual:)* Show must go on!

DOG, VERA, & JO-JO. We go on!

ZETTA. Have a drink!

DOG, VERA, & JO-JO. Don't mind if I do!

ZETTA. Too bad we got no drink, but that'll hold her for now.

JO-JO. TALK TALK TALK FUCK THIS I'M HUNGRY YOU GOT FOOD OR WHAT.

VERA. Yes, yes, my dear, a very good point. *(To ZETTA:)* I must confess a sympathy with Jo-Jo's observation.

ZETTA. We hungry too. Were just about to go hunt when you-all snowed up.

VERA. To cement our new fellowship, allow me to observe that be-fore joining you, we passed a small body of water possibly contain-ing edible wildlife. We will provide, in demonstration of our grati-tude. *(Perhaps producing a small fish spear as if by magic from her clothes.)* Come, Jo-Jo.

> *(VERA and JO-JO exit.)*

ZETTA. Well, well, well! Now we talkin'. What say, José! Back in business and no Miss Snake! Heh, heh, heh-heh-heh! What?

DOG. What?

ZETTA. Don't what me what, what's with? Why all long in the snout?

DOG. Nothing. Reinforcements. Hurray.

ZETTA. Dog, you smell something, you speak. Hear me?

DOG. I hear you, Zetta, but it's nothing.

ZETTA. Yeah?

DOG. Trust me.

> *(Slight pause.)*

ZETTA. Come on. Make a fire case they catch what-all.

> *(They start to build a fire. To herself:)*

Nothing. Nothing, Zetta. Damn-all shut-mouth for a talking dog.

> *(VERA and JO-JO elsewhere on the stage. JO-JO is fish-stalking with concentration.)*

JO-JO. *(Low, maybe continuously until her next line:)* Fish, fish, fish, fish, fish, fish…

VERA. Well, well, well. So far, not entirely without advantageous possibilities. Our new colleagues are certainly very nicely set up. Very nicely indeed. You did well, my dear, in stumbling across them. Such a talented little savage. Still. Finding is one thing. Using is another. Remember what I spoke to you about? Hm? Keep your head, my dear. Are you listening to me, Jo-Jo?

JO-JO. Listening. You want fish?

VERA. I want fish. And I want you to keep that violence of yours in check until it's required. If it's required. There are many ways to exfoliate a feline. Or a canine for that matter.

JO-JO. You know that mutt somewhere before?

VERA. What an extraordinary question. Where would I have known him?

JO-JO. The fuck I know? Got a feeling.

> *(Slight pause.)*

VERA. Fish.

> *(Slight pause.)*

JO-JO. Fish, fish, fish, fish, fish, fish…

> *(Back to the others. They've built a fire.)*

DOG. Zetta?

ZETTA. Uh huh.

DOG. You haven't forgotten about China?

ZETTA. Forget China? Why you ask that? Course not, what kinda dumb-fug question?

DOG. Okay.

ZETTA. Why you think I let these sorry refugees join in? Now we got almost the whole she-bang an magilla, enough bodies for the mortality play and everything. "Forget China."

DOG. Okay.

ZETTA. What-all's biting you, puppy?

DOG. Maybe

ZETTA. Come on, boy. Speak!

DOG. Maybe you're trusting them too fast. Maybe they could be dangerous.

ZETTA. Oh, well. That Jo-Jo got a loose spoke, but she just a little thing. Savvy moolah's on you, push come to gloves, hey?

DOG. Sure.

ZETTA. No change, Dog. You still a headliner. Top-share and all. They good, but they no talkin' dog. You and me, pupster. Walkin' to China. Hey?

DOG. Yeah, sure, Zetta.

>   *(Slight pause. ZETTA begins a slower, a Capella version of their song.)*

ZETTA. DON'T ASK ME WHY

>   *(Slight pause. She starts again:)*

DON'T ASK ME WHY

DOG. DON'T ASK ME WHAT

ZETTA & DOG. DON'T ASK ME NOTHIN' NOTHIN' NOTHIN' NOTHIN' BUT

ZETTA. Tell you one thing: this so-called Vera may be the truth, but she no whole truth so far. "Vaudevillians shall freely exchange all manner of useful info-mation as geographical data, tribal boundaries, recent and on-going armed conflicts and any and all knowledge that may aid a fellow vaudevillian, what-so-never." That the code.

DOG. There's a code?

ZETTA. Why not? So fret not. If she know what-all about the forward route, she be worth fetching along, even with her little loose canon. What?

>   *(DOG has tensed, looking off.)*

DOG. Just them. Smells like they caught something.

>   *(VERA and JO-JO reenter.)*

VERA. Veni vidi vici, my dears. Here is food, or so I hope. I had been led to believe that there are only half a dozen aquatic creatures to be found on our vasty continent, but this asphyxiating fellow is unknown to me.

ZETTA. Now, that a squish.

DOG. *(Sniffing it:)* Edible.

VERA. Jo-Jo will eviscerate. She is deftness itself with a knife. Go on, my dear.

> (JO-JO *pulls out an ugly-looking blade and goes off with the squish.*)

ZETTA. Well, now, then, Vera. Soon's we eat I want to be back on the road. No trade round here 'cept rough trade, and they don't pay. So, what-so-never you know in the way of routes and obstacles, spill now or forever expect no peace.

VERA. But of course, my dear. I am delighted to share what poor scraps of knowledge I've acquired, to further our now combined fortunes. What was your intended destination?

ZETTA. China.

VERA. China?

ZETTA. Chi-na.

VERA. Ah. Yes. On foot?

ZETTA. Not walkin' on our hands.

DOG. We have an engagement.

VERA. Ah.

ZETTA. We been workin' our way north some while now, veering eastward. Out on our usual routes, and we don't know what-alls to come. What's your circuit?

VERA. We were working primarily the South-west to West.

ZETTA. That so? Long time since I been out that way. What the latest?

VERA. Trouble, upheaval, dark, dark times. The Lone Star Libertarian Army is attempting another invasion of the Pan-AmerIndian Casino Nation.

ZETTA. Again? Stubborn sons, got to give 'em that.

VERA. Naturally, they're quite doomed. Casino Nation possesses Technology, you know.

ZETTA. Sure. Played there once with my Mam's troupe when I was coming up. Never forget it. Lec-trixity, Dog.

VERA. Can you imagine that, Dog?

DOG. No.

(*Slight pause.*)

VERA. Well. Ever since the Nuevo Aztecs ejected them from what used to be called Texas, the Lone Stars have been, how shall I say? martially resistant to historical trends. Despite the inequality of the struggle, it has dragged on long enough to wreak bloody havoc, and our fragile little troupe was caught in the crossfire. Casino Nation's Technology being both deadly and none so accurate, it was perhaps not surprising, however distressing, that we came under friendly fire — that ancient ironic phrase — and lost half our players in one fiery blast. And our cart with all its precious cargo.

ZETTA. (*Softly swearing:*) Jesse fug-it Crisco.

VERA. Indeed. Clearly, there was no safety to be had in the entire region, and no great demand for our noble art. So we buried what we could find of our fallen comrades, shouldered the remnants of our belongings, and steered our course due north, hopeful of mended fortunes. We perambulated fearlessly as far as the very shadow of the Great Canadian Barrier Wall, but, alas, we soon found ourselves performing only the clichéd fire/frying pan scenario. The tribes of the Mid North and North-West are unspeakably diverse and dangerously agnostic regarding the sacred person of the Vaudevillian. Radical-Agrarian-Utopians. Paranoic-UFO-Communing-Separatists. The Skinhead-Skateboarders Union. Millennial-Revisionists.

ZETTA. Never heard on 'em.

VERA. Oh, yes, they're quite fascinating. They refuse to believe the Apocalypse has come and gone, it having failed their expectations, and every year their priests solemnly postpone the deadline. Well, as I previously related, our career reached its nadir when we lost the surviving male members of our troupe to the procreational demands of the sisters *sans merci*. All told, by the time we'd emerged into the blessed wilderness of the blasted East, we were as you find us: sans troupe, sans props, sans cart, sans very nearly everything.

(JO-JO comes back with skinned and gutted squish on a stick. DOG goes to take it from her. She recoils, holds up the knife.)

JO-JO. *(Hissing at him:)* Ssssss

VERA. Jo-Jo.

DOG. *(To* JO-JO:*)* It's all right. I was just helping. We have a fire, see?

VERA. Give it to him, Jo-Jo.

DOG. It's all right. You cook it.

> *(He retreats.* JO-JO *goes to the fire, holds the squish over it.)*

JO-JO. *(Muttering:)* I fucking caught it.

VERA. If I may, Zetta, be so bold as to venture a query…

ZETTA. What-all, speak free.

VERA. You referred earlier to a Dog Act. I have heard, as who has not? of this fabled wonder of the dim and glorious past, but I have never been privileged to witness one, dogs in general being so sadly declined and brutish in our jaded age. I confess it, I burn with vulgar curiosity.

ZETTA. Hey now, fair enough. Dog don't mind, hey, Dog? Hey? Dog?

DOG. My throat's a little hoarse. From the smoke.

ZETTA. Oh, now, that don't matter. Do the short version. *(To* VERA:*)* It one hell of an act, never fail. *(To* DOG:*)* Come on there, Dog, snazzle us all ready.

> *(DOG mounts the stage of the cart, and stands for a moment facing upstage.)*

ZETTA. Oh, you in for something now. Some places, we can't barely pull the cart for what-all they throw at us, after they catch an earload a Dog there.

> *(DOG turns, and speaks in grand heightened Shakespearian style infused with deep feeling.)*

DOG. Doubt that the earth quakes. Doubt that the sun shivers and flares. Doubt that the moon broke free of our doubtful gravity to fall endlessly into the endless night, but never doubt that I am yours and more constant than earth, sun or treacherous moon. Can words encompass my love? Shall I debase the immaculate ardor of a perfect flame to say "I love you?" Don't listen to my words. Words can lie, words are made for betrayal, the same word may issue from the mouth of a saint and a villain. Listen to your own heart, beating in rhythm with mine. It will tell you what is in my heart, for two hearts as one can keep no secrets. You are the air I breathe, the life's blood in my veins, you are every thought and dream and longing that shake this poor frame, weak with groaning for you, with not sleeping for calling your name. You are love itself and I am your slave. You are life itself and I worship you. Don't speak, never speak, and I may wait for ever in the exquisite hope of your love and never know the torment of being cast out of your light. I love you. I love you. I love you.

> (DOG *bows.* VERA *and* ZETTA *applaud.* ZETTA *tears a strip off the cooking squish and tosses it to* DOG, *who pops it into his mouth and comes off the stage.)*

ZETTA. Good boy. Good dog.

VERA. Amazing. One would almost believe he actually understands what he's saying.

ZETTA. *(Patting him:)* Who a good dog?

DOG. I am.

ZETTA. *(To* VERA:) How about that, hey? Ever seen what-all to beat that, hey?

VERA. Never.

ZETTA. Never what-all. Well, now, then. Where we at. You got nothing on the North-East road, then?

VERA. Well, nothing recent. But I was once very familiar with these parts. Intimately familiar. You've never come this far?

ZETTA. Said not.

VERA. Not even your Dog there? Perhaps before he joined your enterprise?

ZETTA. He'd a said if so. Hey, Dog?

DOG. I would have said.

ZETTA. Why you ask?

VERA. Merely seeking clarification on the point. Well. Many years ago, not far from here, there was a small tribe living in the fortified remnants of what used to be a sort of…cathedral.

ZETTA. Cath-e-dral?

VERA. An ancient place of worship. But this was a secular cathedral. For the worship of knowledge. When I knew them, they were a benign people. Making their home among the books. They could all read. Imagine that. And they were safe. Marauding savages would come to the gates, but the gates were strong, and the walls were high and the place easily defended. They were happy enough, as the world goes.

ZETTA. Sounds like people might appreciate a show. How far? Could you find it?

VERA. Not far. It's on the way to the sea. And I'm entirely certain I could never forget the way, however long ago I last saw it.

ZETTA. Damn-all this stop-still, then, let's move! Eat walking, come on there, girl, put out the fire. Dog, shake it, pack up, let's go!

(Another violent earth-wobble.)

ALL. WOOOOOH!

(They all fall down. It's suddenly very hot, and everyone begins stripping off outer layers.)

ZETTA. Summer! Fug-hat! Where-all spring?

JO-JO. Hot hot HOT!

VERA. Ah, grateful warmth.

ZETTA. Come 'ere, Jo, I'll show you where to stow your stuff and all.

> (DOG *in the front of the cart pulls the harness over his shoulders.* VERA *moves closer to him, unobserved by* ZETTA *who is helping* JO-JO *in the back.*)

VERA. I know you.

DOG. No.

VERA. Oh, yes, perfectly. Just as perfectly as you remember me.

DOG. I don't. Leave me alone.

ZETTA. *(Coming back around:)* All ready, hey? Then lead on, Mizz Duff! An audience awaits! Play us off, Dog.

> (*They pull the cart around in a circle and off,* DOG *in harness and playing a steady beat, all singing singing "The Wang-tailed Wallow" as a walking song. As soon as they're gone,* COKE *and* BUD *enter, looking after them.*)

BUD. Fuck this, for-fuckin-sooth, let us fuck off home. My feet are fucked.

COKE. Hast no fucking guts? That's our fucking prize.

BUD. Art thy eyes and ears be-fucked? They're fucking vaudevillians.

COKE. So fucking what? And watch thy tongue.

BUD. Watch it for me, thou fuck-sucking cunt-roach, dost think I shut up at thy fucking decree?

COKE. Not now, not now, not fucking now, I'm trying to fucking think.

BUD. Oh, fuck this then, we'll be here till we're fucking bones.

COKE. That's it, thou'rt fucked.

> (COKE *applies some form of violent suppression to* BUD.)

BUD. Ah, fuck.

COKE. Dost hear me now, thou limp-dickied would-be sister-fucker?

BUD. Ay.

COKE. Then attend. One: why should these fucking vaudevillians be not fair game and sport for a bold scavenger? Who should say me fucking nay if I choose?

BUD. Our divine leader protector and mother of us all THE WENDY, thou fucking freak, that's fucking who—

COKE. Ah, ah, wouldst speak with that tongue?

BUD. Thorry, thorry. *(COKE lets go of his tongue.)* And yet, if thou will hear me…they're off-fucking-limits. The Wendy forbids it. Fuck knows why, but it's always been so.

COKE. *(Getting up:)* Wendy's fucked, isn't she? Dead and gone and broken up to spare fucking parts, Praise Her Usefulness.

COKE & BUD. Praise it. Wendy's Here To Stay.

BUD. But there'll be a new one, soon as someone scrounges her up. That's what we ought to be looking for, not footling afar after one scrawny runt of a ratty prize that's taboo to boot.

COKE. Not so scrawny. And I fucking caught it, dost hear? My fucking prizes stay fucking caught or what the fuck am I? As for so-called taboo, that brings me to two. Two: The rest of them may be fucking vaudevillians. But that prize is none.

BUD. What means thou? We saw its fucking act. It sucked squirrel anus, but—

COKE. It's been trained, what the fuck does that prove? It's been with them long enough, but it didn't start out with them. Dids't mark its cleverness? Fuck, it got away from me. From me!

BUD. And me.

COKE. And boosted our boodle on the fly! I fucking say it—it's one of ours. It's a born scavenger, and fuck me bloody if I don't get it back or break its neck trying.

BUD. Well but if it's one of ours, we can't fucking eat it, can we? So what's the fucking point?

COKE. If thy fucking head weren't full of fucking shit thy fucking skull would collapse. It's female, right?

BUD. Ahh…

COKE. Fucking right, ah. It's too small for a Wendy, but I know where it would fit. Ah? Ah?

COKE & BUD. *(Roaring lewdly:)*AARRHH!

BUD. What are we fucking around for, then, let's fucking after it!

COKE. Easy, easy, for fuck's sake. The prize took our fucking weapons, dost remember?

BUD. Fuck, right, yeah. Fuck. And there's but we two against… *(Concentrating, counting on his fingers, then giving up:)* more of them.

COKE. And one a fucking dog. Fuck it, by thy mother's tits, the taboo fits not a fucking dog. I'll take my chances with the next Wendy—I'll have that hound's heart in my belly before the seasons change, the fuck I won't.

BUD. It looked a fierce mean dog, withal. Oh, yeah, but fuck it, I'm with thee! Fuck, yeah!

COKE. Come on, then, but keep thy fucking tongue still, or I'll have it for a fucking garnish. We'll follow apace, and watch our moment.

(They exit.)

End of Act I

ACT II

(From off we hear a drum beat, a steady walking rhythm, and then the VAUDEVILLIANS singing "The Wang-tailed Wallow." They enter, pulling the cart. VERA is walking in front. She stops and the others stop singing. There's a brief silence, as they all take in the ruins before them.)

ZETTA. Sad old place, this.

VERA. Indeed.

ZETTA. Grievous old ju-ju went on here. Anything, Dog? Dog.

DOG. What?

ZETTA. What you smell?

DOG. I don't know.

VERA. Old smoke. Long-spilt blood. Treachery, catastrophe, death. Even my poor nose can smell that much in these ruins.

ZETTA. Well, what-ever-all this is, it be nothing to us. Let's get on, hey? Think we can make your cath-ee-drell by dark? Hey? Vera? Damn-all, everybody turn to stone here?

VERA. I beg your pardon, my dear. I was adrift in bitter nostalgia. For I must inform you, to my infinite regret, that we have reached our destination.

ZETTA. No. This-all? This rubble? Fug-hat, this it? Hang on, now, this dev-no-station old and old. Weeds are well-grown to bury all. Whatever disaster came down on here was long ago.

VERA. So it seems. I did say, it was long ago that I last was here.

ZETTA. You did say. Must have followed fast upon your exit. Guess you did well to leave.

VERA. I did well to live. Many here did not, by the look of it. See, where the window frames are splintered, and blackened by soot? A savage fury tore this place apart stone by stone, and burnt what could burn. What would we find, do you think, if we were to wander amongst the ruins and dig, just a little, among the choking vines? A single shoe? Rain-rotten pages of what were books, rewritten now by weather and ignorance? Bones, do you think? Surely we would find bones, lying, sinking into the yielding dirt, where people fell. Where they died. Their terrible, surprising deaths. When the walls were finally breached. Or however it happened.

DOG. *(Quietly:)* Zetta. Let's walk on.

ZETTA. All right, there, Vera. We walking on bones every day we walk the earth. This a bad place, sure, and I disappointed too, but what be, be, and old news is nothing to us here and now, 'cept we got to think of what next. It be dark soon. And the unknown road's the darkest, they say. Better sleep here and start fresh.

DOG. Let's walk on, Zetta, please.

ZETTA. Well, que pasa, Dog? You know something I ought to? *(He doesn't answer.)* You just spooked, pupster. Wore out from a long haul. Make no sense what-all to keep on now, hey? Lookit, you rest up, I'll take Jo-thing to gather firewood.

DOG. No, I'm not tired. I'll come with you.

ZETTA. *(Looks at him. Then, to VERA:)* We going for wood. You-all make camp.

VERA. Avec plaisir, mon capitane.

> *(ZETTA and DOG exit. JO-JO pulls her bag off the cart and pulls out a weapon, sits on the ground and begins to sharpen, oil or otherwise refurbish it. VERA opens the cart and begins to explore the contents.)*

VERA. Instruments, of an unusual nature. Costumes. Bedding. Hmm, books. I would have wagered our intrepid leader was fully as literate as a squish. Perhaps she enjoys perusing the illustrations. …Very nice. Very old. And what have we here? Fascinating. Quite a collection of ancient artifacts. By the looks of it, the contents of this cart have been passed down through many a generation. A true aristocrat of the trade, our Zetta. What are you doing, Jo-Jo?

JO-JO. Nothin'.

VERA. I don't remember that weapon.

JO-JO. It's mine.

VERA. Jo-Jo. Where did it come from?

JO-JO. It's mine. I found it.

> (VERA *comes down off the cart.*)

VERA. Jo-Jo. I asked you before, and now I think, true to your name, you were less than truthful with me: when you went missing those few hours, the other day. And came back scratched and bruised.

JO-JO. Fell asleep ina tree. Fell out.

VERA. Look at me, Jo-Jo.

JO-JO. Fell. Fell outa tree.

VERA. Look at me.

JO-JO. (*Leaping up and raising weapon:*) FELL OUTA FUCKIN TREE.

> (VERA *looks at* JO-JO *steadily and speaks slowly, never raising her voice.*)

VERA. A little liar. But not a good one. I can see right through you. Right through you, Jo-Jo. I can see right through you.

> (JO-JO *has slowly lowered the weapon, intimidated by* VERA.)

Where did the weapon come from, Jo-Jo?

JO-JO. Took it.

VERA. From whom, Jo-Jo?

JO-JO. Scavengers.

> (*Slight pause.*)

VERA. Scavengers.

JO-JO. They caught me. Went to take a pee, fuckin' caught me. But I got away. They were stupid. Hah. I got away, and I took their stuff. See?

> (*She holds the bag open to show* VERA.)

See? Gotta whole buncha their stuff. Hah.

VERA. And you're very pleased and proud, aren't you? To have scavenged a Scavenger?

JO-JO. Two of 'em.

VERA. You unspeakable little half-wit. One, two, an army of Scavengers. What they find, they do not relinquish. Recycle, reclaim and reuse, but never, never relinquish. You belong to them now, you troglodytic wretch.

JO-JO. No.

VERA. Yes, my dear, you are lawful Scavenger prize. No doubt they have been tracking you ever since. This is an unwelcome development. You might have told me sooner.

JO-JO. I'm not theirs. I have their weapons. I'll fuckin' kill them.

VERA. Yes, yes, you're the fiercest creature in the forest, I know. Well, after all, there may be a way to turn this to our advantage.

JO-JO. I'm with you now. I'm a vauder now. You said.

VERA. All right, all right, there, there. I know what it is to take refuge in an assumed identity. We neither of us were born to the life, but for a long time now it has been a haven to me, and served my turn, and it will yet for both of us. I don't suppose you're prepared at last to explain your origins to me? Whence you sprang, before I found you that long-ago day?

JO-JO. Told you. Don't remember.

VERA. And that may even be true. Enough for now. I must think. Keep your eyes open, hm? And that evil-looking object at the ready.

> (VERA *goes back into the cart, while* JO-JO *stands guard. Elsewhere on the stage* ZETTA *is binding together a large bundle of branches with strips of cloth or leather.* DOG *is nearby, maybe lying on the ground like a sick dog.*)

ZETTA. Hey. Hey, Dog. Smell that? Maybe…yeah, there he be. That the sea, Dog. I knew we getting close. Man, oh man, if that ain't the smell of all change nor possibility. I ever tell you, Dog, the one time I smell the sea? Ever tell you that one? Long and long ago. Back in the day when it my mam's cart, and we a dozen strong almost. Oh, we could make an entrance then, razz and dazz, tribe knew it when we came in. I had three daddies then, Dog, Mam's three men. Sword-swaller, acro-gnat and the little old odd-jobber, who sewed costumes, pulled teeth need be, cooked, mixed medicines, whatever-all. Clever son. They all nice to me, but I remember him most, some reason. Mam's busy, running things, but Jemmy had time for me. Well so Mam always kept us inland, said there's plenty land to keep us working, no need to get too close the edge, where who knows? Might wind up on a piece ready to fall off. Said sea's a treacherous critter, never trust him. Said sea's always nagging at the land, biting and tugging, and jumpin' up and over. Said there's tribe and tribe used to be, now lying under, deep and deep. And that's true enough, Dog. It's in the books. You know that, Dog? Well. One time, we were out on our usual circuit by a few days, detouring for a tribal offshoot wanted us specially, celebrate making it through the first year on their own. Way and away down south and west. High summer, plenty to eat, nice tribe. Day after day they kept us on. Everybody happy. Good gig. But day we going to leave, all a sudden, wind changed. Blew up wet and strange from the south. Jem smelled it. Next thing, he packed up separate and ready to walk. Mam so pissed, but nothing she can do. She worked on him, talking herself blue. All he said, he'd come from down there, down by the sea, and now he smelled it again, he had to see it too. Just had to. Said it was pulling and tugging and he had to go. You ever felt like that, anything, Dog? Well so maybe we sat and talked and maybe it all took days, but way I remember, that was it for Jem. He walked away and kept on walking, and we watched him walk, and that the end on it. Mam told me it was because he wasn't a true roadster. She said, one of those things you can't help. Where you belong got a gravity and it going to pull you hard. But fug-hat, Dog. Why this sea-smell making me think? I followed Jem a ways. But Mam was right. I went back, and we went away back inland. Maybe, though, nothing was the same. And one by one company died or got ate or went off and started new companies. Mam died with half the others, that drought summer when we had to drink what we could find, and it bad water, turned out. Well. All that long ago, and we doing fine and fine. Hey, Dog? So this stop-over a slosh-out, we got the gig of gigs ahead. King of China'll lavish us with rewards be-fitting and laissez le bon ton roulez once more. You know it, Dog. We better shake out the Play with the new hires, scrape off the rust, hey? Polish her up. Been a while. Wish I knew what eating you, damn-all if I don't.

Look up there, Dog. Getting dark down here, but sky still fat with light, glowing all kind colors. Something, hey? Wicked old world, but she ours.

(VERA is lighting lanterns, JO-JO completing a fire-circle of rocks. The stage of the cart has been folded out and some cushions arranged on it.)

VERA. I want you to take whatever opportunity may present itself, Jo-Jo, to sequester our benefactress some little while. I need a quiet word with the two-legged mongrel. Given the possibly imminent invasion by your savage acquaintances, I can no longer afford to take my time as I might prefer, pursuant to our aims. Acceleration seems advisable. Do you understand?

JO-JO. Get mizz Zetta away so you can work the dog.

VERA. A fair approximation.

(ZETTA & DOG return with bundles of sticks, which they dump beside the fire-circle.)

ZETTA. Make the fire there, okay, Jo-girl?

DOG. I'll do it.

ZETTA. No, Dog. You sickening for something. Go lie down. I said, go lie down, Dog.

You can make a fire all right, hey, Jo-critter?

JO-JO. Course I can.

ZETTA. Okay, then.

(Leaves her to it, goes up to VERA. They look at the sky.)

Look clear enough what-all, hey?

VERA. Assuredly. And yet, I don't quite like that yellow in the north-west. In my experience, it is an ill portent.

ZETTA. Can be. But no wind. Maybe we get wet sometime tomorrow, but nothing to fret over.

VERA. Agreed. Barring unexpected shifts, our night, at least, will be calm.

JO-JO *(Low, starting the fire:)* Fire, fire, fire, fire, fire, fire, fire. *(It lights.)* Fire.

> *(VERA goes and sits by the fire with JO-JO. ZETTA gets out a small sack of smoked squish, gives some to DOG.)*

ZETTA. Here, Dog.

> *(He takes it, but doesn't eat. She comes and joins the others around the fire. The little sack of food gets passed around as they speak.)*

Vera, should have asked before. These people used to be here, they friends of yours?

VERA. One could say so.

ZETTA. Long time ago. But tray desolay. My sympathy, and what-all, you know.

VERA. Thank you.

> *(Slight pause.)*

ZETTA. Damn-all hot, still. Just when you ready for a season-change, she turn stubborn, hey? Get stuck on summer who know how long.

VERA. Quite.

> *(Slight pause.)*

ZETTA. Good fire, Jo-thing.

> *(Slight pause.)*

Say now, Jo-ster, what say you give us another out on your repertoire, hey?

Night for a story, if ever.

> *(Again, JO-JO launches instantly into her story-telling mode.)*

JO-JO. "ONCE IN THE LONG AGO TIME there were two brothers, one was Coyote and one was Gopher, one day when Coyote was off hunting an old woman came to the brothers' tent where Gopher was sitting in the sun, the old woman said I am thirsty, Gopher said there is no water, old woman said I am hungry, Gopher said there is no food, old woman said I am tired let me rest in your tent, Gopher said go away old woman there is nothing here for you, old woman then became what she was, that was a wolf, Gopher ran away but Wolf caught him and ate him in two bites, when Coyote came home from hunting a young woman was sitting in front of his tent, where is Gopher? he asked, the woman did not answer, he looked at her and he desired her, she said I am thirsty, he gave her water, she stayed, after many years he woke one night and she was not in the tent, he went out but he could not see her, all he heard were wolves howling, the next day he said to her I woke in the night and you were not here, she said you dreamed, he said no where were you? she said you dreamed husband do not ask me anymore, Coyote became angry then but he said nothing, that night he pretended to sleep, in the night she went out, he followed, she became what she was, that was a wolf, he saw her HE SAW HER."

(*She's finished.*)

ZETTA. Well? What happens next?

JO-JO. Don't know. How it ends.

(*They sit in silence for a moment. Then* ZETTA *begins singing softly, to the tune of* Swing Low Sweet Chariot:)

ZETTA. SING YO, STREET HARRIET
COMIN' FOUR O'CLOCK TO MY DOOR
SING YO, STREET HARRIET
COME IN FOR THE FOUR O'CLOCK SHOW

(VERA *joins in.*)

ZETTA & VERA. I LOOKED OVER WANDA
AND WHAT DID I SEE
COMIN' FOUR O'CLOCK TO MY DOOR?
A BAND OF WASTRELS
SHOOTIN' UP AT THREE
COMIN' FOR THE FOUR O'CLOCK SHOW

(JO-JO joins in. Three-part harmony if possible.)

ZETTA, VERA & JO-JO. SLING JOE, FLEET CHERRY-ANNE
COMIN' FOUR OR FIVE ON THE FLOOR
SLING JOE, FLEET CHERRY-ANNE
COMMISSAR DON'T WANT YOU NO MORE

ZETTA. Now, that an old one, for sure and all.

VERA. One of the oldest.

JO-JO. Still hungry.

ZETTA. I did see some berry bushes, getting the wood. Could pick some in the dark, maybe.

JO-JO. *(Getting a look from VERA:)* Oh. Um. Yeah. I'll help you. Let's go. C'mon.

ZETTA. Well, there, Jo-girl, coming out on your shell, aren't ya? Sure, what-ever-all, let's go get some berries. Bring that lantern.

DOG. Zetta.

ZETTA. We be back in a jump-jack-flash, Dog. Stay.

(ZETTA and JO-JO exit. Slight pause.)

VERA. Strange, isn't it? It must be perfectly surreal, not to say nightmarish, for you, finding yourself here again, after so long. It's strange enough for me. Quite numbingly painful, even for me, at first.

DOG. I don't. I don't know what. What you.

VERA. It's possible, I grant, that you don't remember me. You were young. Still of an age to find most adults interchangeable. I slept on the far side of the, what did we call it? The campus. I think it was over there, my tower. Though it's curiously difficult to get my bearings. It's so much altered. The place where we both were born. Where I grew up, worked, made plans. Till the sky fell and everything ended.

DOG. I've never. Been here. Never seen. You. Or this. Place.

VERA. Do you not remember who I am? Now, I mean to say, who

I am now. I cannot lie. I tell only the truth. Not the whole truth, but nothing but the truth. You may not remember me. But I know you. I know what you did, boy.

(*Slight pause.*)

DOG. Are you going to kill me?

VERA. Is that what you want?

DOG. It doesn't matter.

VERA. Are you inviting me to pity you?

DOG. No.

VERA. How did it happen, precisely? I've so often wondered.

Am I not entitled to know?

DOG. I wanted to know. What was outside the walls. Everyone said terrible things. But I knew that grown-ups didn't always tell the truth. I didn't believe them. I wanted to know. So I slipped away. I went to the South Gate. I knew the watchman that time and day was my uncle Fig. I knew he got sleepy after lunch. I waited till he dozed off and I opened the gate. I only meant to look. But there was that little ridge, that I couldn't see over. I found I had to just see what was on the other side. And there were woods, and there was something through the trees, and I found I just had to go see what that was. It was stream, running off down a slope, and I followed it. After I'd walked for a while I got tired, and I lay among some ferns to rest. And I fell asleep. When I woke up it was nearly dark. I was worried. I'd have been missed by then. How would I explain? I followed the stream back, and went through the little woods, and climbed up the ridge. I began to hear a noise. I came to the top of the ridge.

VERA. You'd left the gate open.

DOG. I'd left the gate open.

How did you survive?

VERA. Some of the women they didn't kill.

I often, later, wondered what became of you.

DOG. I became a dog.

My mother. Was she.

VERA. She fought too valiantly to be captured. An arrow pierced her brain, through an eye.

DOG. Didn't you fight too?

VERA. Oh, no. I surrendered instantly. By the end of the first day's captivity I was the slave of the head-man. At the end of a week, he was mine. I wasn't beautiful, mind you.

DOG. I know what you were.

VERA. Are you judging me?

DOG. No.

VERA. Surely it isn't necessary to remind you.

DOG. No.

VERA. It is strange, being here again. If I didn't know better, I would say there's a feeling here of unquiet ghosts. Do you feel that? Restless spirits of the betrayed and unavenged.

DOG. They. They wouldn't have wanted.

VERA. Wouldn't have wanted revenge? They were a gentle people. But they were most ungently served. No doubt you imagine that your own suffering, your voluntary demotion from humanity, your assumption of canine humility are sufficient to shield you from your own past deeds. It doesn't work that way, dear boy, as you ought to know. It is a matter of consequences. Not a moral question at all. There are things that forgiveness cannot touch. There are things that once done cannot be undone. Do you understand me? Feeling any amount of guilt or anguish, performing any little rites of expiation, all that is quite beside the point, because it isn't a sin, a personal moral drama — it is an historical fact. A miniature civilization lies here in ruins and decay. Because of you. I stand here as the sole survivor of your act of thoughtlessness and selfishness. The sole surviving member of your own tribe. Your only kin in this world, and your victim. Can you look at me and deny me anything? Can you look at me and not know that you belong to me, body and, for what it's worth, soul?

DOG. No.

VERA. That's right.

I'm glad we've had this chance to talk. I'm sure it's a relief to you, in a way. You've come home. All you need do now is remember where your allegiance lies. I won't ask anything else from you. Do you understand me, Dog?

DOG. Yes.

>   *(We hear* ZETTA *and* JO-JO *returning.*)*

VERA. Do you, Dog?

DOG. Yes, Vera.

JO-JO. *(*Beginning off, continuing as they enter:)* And y' never eat the white ones, or the red ones, or the black ones, or the yellow ones, or the orange ones, just the blue ones, right, or the purple ones, or the big red ones, but not the little red ones, right, cause the little red ones'll kill you but good and the black ones'll —

>   *(They've entered the camp by now, and seeing* VERA *and* DOG, *JO-JO falls silent.)*

ZETTA. That's right, Jo-girl, you got berries down stone. Hey, now, Dog, feeling a tad better? Hey, Vera. Berries for all. People here must of cult-no-vated them, more than we can pick if we picked all night.

VERA. A very welcome addition to our repast. Good work, Jo-Jo.

ZETTA. Here, pupster, eat something. We ate plenty while picking. Never foraged in the dark before, but Jo-girl's got sharp eyes on her, could be a nowl of old.

>   *(DOG takes the berries offered, but doesn't eat.)*

JO-JO. Nowl?

ZETTA. Nowls were big fierce bad old birds, could see in the dark an fly silent, pick off anything came out at night. If you too big to eat, they ask: Who? Who? And then watch out, cause nowls harbingers of death.

JO-JO. Harb-a-gers?

VERA. Forerunner sign messenger outrider warning herald.

ZETTA. First you see nowl, soon next you going to see death come up say: "hey."

Who? Whoooo.

JO-JO. HEY. HEY.

ZETTA. *(Laughing:)* Hey there, Jo-ster, easy up. No nowls round here.

VERA. Not for a long, long time. Have you ever seen one, Dog?

Have you ever seen an owl, Dog?

DOG. No, Vera.

ZETTA. Well, now, there, Vera. Thinking. About time we took the Play out for a spin, see how she fits with the new group. Hey? Early yet, may as well rehearse before weather changes on us again.

VERA. That, my dear, is a perfectly marvelous conception. We stand ready.

ZETTA. All right then. Set-up!

> *(A flurry of activity ensues, as costumes are put on, props and costume changes laid out, musical instruments checked, tuned and readied, non-essential items like the berries tidied away. Jo-Jo's bag containing the scavenger's weapons ends up to the side of the cart, upstage. As this begins,* VERA *takes the opportunity to speak to* JO-JO *in an aside:)*

VERA. I have muzzled the mutt. Now is the time to act. You will find your moment and give our brave vaudevillian the hook, at the point of your knife.

JO-JO. Vera. How come. I mean. Why not. I mean.

VERA. Have you an objection, Jo-Jo?

JO-JO. Why we can't just go like we are? With Zetta? She and Dog. They not so bad.

VERA. *(Rapidly:)* I would have thought even your small wit could have puzzled that out without a pause for exposition. But, attend, I will illumine: we have lost our cart and everything we need to live; Zetta will share, up to a point, but it is her cart and her properties and her sufferance; they could chase us off whenever they pleased, and we would revert instantly to desperate need; not to mention that I am no one's supporting player. It is true that I could take it all, but slowly, so she would not know at what moment it ceases to be hers and becomes mine; I could enslave her, as I have her mongrel, without spilling a salty droplet. I have done it before. But I am no longer as patient as I once was, I am not patient at all and I will have it, I will take it, I will not wait. Marauders are at the gate again and we must be ready. So. Yes? Do you understand? May we go on now? When we come to The Tower scene, when you come on as the plagues, switch the prop knife: let your blade be real, and let it be swift. The dog won't hinder you. Then when your Scavengers show up they can have her body to recycle. Instead of yours. Go on, now. Prepare.

> *(The preparations continue and now* ZETTA *and* DOG *speak apart.)*

ZETTA. Give me a hand with this, hey, Dog? This just what-all you need; you be a new critter with the show-juices flowing again. Long time since we done the thing all the way through.

DOG. Zetta, listen, there are things. There are things you don't. Listen there are things you don't know about me.

ZETTA. No kidding. You picking this moment out of a blizzardness of moments to spill a revelation? Hey? Well, okay, snoops, spill away.

> *(DOG doesn't speak.)*

Now, you listen a me, pup. Speak, don't speak, it your own story to tell or keep shut-mouth on. You know me, I want to know any-all info-mation going, add it to the stockpile. But fug-hat, if it be the past wigging you out, my advice? Make your peace and move along. History's a bitch to have at your heels. Smell that sweet old night, Dog? Feel that old earth of ours underfoot? Enough, can't it be? Okay, all

I'm saying, you got to figure it out your own self. For me, you my dog and I take you as you are, don't need the back-story, nevermind the pedigree and filigree and narrative hoo-hah. Hey? Okay then.

> *(She moves off about her tasks. DOG looks after her. JO-JO sidles up.)*

JO-JO. Sorry.

DOG. What?

JO-JO. I'm sorry.

DOG. Why?

> *(Slight pause.)*

JO-JO. FUCK OFF aright JUST FUCK OFF

ZETTA. Hey, hey, got the jittabugs there, Jo-thing? C'mere, let's get you set up. I got your prop knife for the Tower, c'mon, now.

> *(JO-JO goes upstage to ZETTA. VERA speaks aside to DOG.)*

VERA. Our little liar is volatile, but you needn't fear her. She is a weapon that I have the aiming of, and the trigger.

DOG. Are you aiming her at Zetta?

VERA. What is that to you? You don't belong to her anymore. Your silence proves it. You would have told her everything by now if you were still hers. But you don't speak, because you know very well that if she knew what you are, she would, very rightly, no longer trust you. She would hold you in contempt. Anyway, she isn't of your tribe. I am. Remember that, and no harm will come to you.

ZETTA. Well now so, think we all good to go here. Stop if need be, but let's try to get right through her in one gallop, hey? Get the feel of her. Places! Hit it, Dog.

> *(DOG begins to play, and the others take their places. There is a brief—no more than a minute or two—opening number/overture here. For example, if the actors have skills such as juggling, tumbling, stilt walking, etc., these could be displayed simultaneously. Or they could play and sing a medley of snippets from the three*

songs we've already heard. Then ZETTA *comes forward.)*

ZETTA. Listen all and you shall hear
A tale to make you quake with fear
A story full of woe and pity
The rise and fall of human-ity
The breathless rise and tragic fall
Of those before who made us all
Listen well, and learn once more
The misery that lies in store
For those who will forget the past
May perish in a fiery blast
Listen well but blame us not
It was not we who wrote the plot
Have mercy on we players poor
If we offend, forbear to roar
And if you roar, forbear to rage
Remember all the world's a stage
We do our best, look you do too
Or we will in our turn judge you

> *(Exeunt to music. While everyone is occupied, we see the Scavengers sneak on upstage, steal back the bag of weapons and exit. A painted sign is revealed, reading; "Act 1: Adam and Eve's Evolutionary Comedy." VERA and JO-JO step forward with a musical introduction played by DOG or ZETTA.)*

VERA / ADAM. Say, Eve, what's all this I hear about the origin of the species?

JO-JO / EVE. Say, Adam, glad you asked. It's all very simple. First came Who, an amoeba, and then came What, a fish, and third, I Don't Know crawled onto land and grew feet. See?

VERA / ADAM. What a minute, wait a minute. Who came first?

JO-JO / EVE. That's right. Who came first.

VERA / ADAM. That's what I'm asking.

JO-JO / EVE. Who.

VERA / ADAM. You tell me.

JO-JO / EVE. I'm telling you.

VERA / ADAM. Who?!

JO-JO / EVE. That's right, Who!

VERA / ADAM. You tell me!

JO-JO / EVE. Okay, hold on now —

VERA / ADAM. Jeez!

JO-JO / EVE. It's simple, Adam, now listen. What came next.

VERA / ADAM. What?

JO-JO / EVE. That's right.

VERA / ADAM. WHAT?

JO-JO / EVE. A fish! And who crawled onto the land and grew feet?

VERA / ADAM. I don't know!

JO-JO / EVE. That's right! I Don't Know!

VERA / ADAM. One of these days, Eve! Bang, zoom! To the moon!

(DOG *enters as the snake, juggling apples.*)

DOG / SNAKE. Say, Adam and Eve, ya hear the one about the origin of the species?

VERA & JO-JO. *(Turning on him:)* Aw, shaddup!

DOG / SNAKE. Awright, awright! *(Offering an apple:)* Anybody hungry?

> (VERA *and* JO-JO *haul off to smack* DOG, *who ducks so they clock each other instead; a slapstick fight ensues, with* ZETTA *doing comic sound-effects. Finally* DOG *takes a big bite of an apple;* ZETTA *makes a loud, ominous sound-effect like thunder; the other three look up to the sky anxiously. Then* ZETTA *plays a flourish of exit music, they jump up, bow and run off. A new sign appears, reading: "Act 2: Rozetta Stone sings The Human Blues." During the song — if not before — unnoticed by the players, the Scavengers creep in downstage and sit watching.)*

ZETTA. CRITTER IN THE BUSHES, CRITTER IN THE SKY
DON'T KNOW NOTHING, THEY JUST LIVE AND THEY DIE
CRITTER IN THE RIVER, CRITTER IN THE SEA
DON'T KNOW NOTHING AND THEY HAPPIER THAN ME
I KNOW ONE THING, KNOW IT CHAPTER AND VERSE
HOWEVER BAD IT BEEN, IT GONNA KEEP GETTING WORSE
I GOT THE HUMAN BLUES
O-O-O-OH THE HUMAN BLUES

THE APPLE OF EDEN IS A SOUR OLD FRUIT
FILLED WITH BITTER WISDOM FROM THE TWIG TO THE
        ROOT
THAT APPLE IT LEAVE AN EVIL TASTE IN THE MOUTH
ONCE IT GET IN IT AIN'T NEVER GET OUT
I KNOW ONE THING, KNOW IT UPSIDE AND DOWN
WHEN THE WATER RISE, EVERYBODY GET DROWN
I GOT THE HUMAN BLUES
O-O-O-OH THE HUMAN BLUES

KNOW ENOUGH TO MUTTER, KNOW ENOUGH TO MOAN
KNOW ENOUGH TO KNOW I CAN'T NEVER GO HOME
KNOW ENOUGH TO HOLLER, KNOW ENOUGH TO HOWL
KNOW ENOUGH TO KNOW I KNOW NOTHING AT ALL
I KNOW ONE THING, GOT IT NAILED TO THE FLOOR
ALTHOUGH IT DO ME NO GOOD, I ALWAYS GOT TO KNOW
        MORE
I GOT THE HUMAN BLUES
O-O-O-OH THE HUMAN BLUES

>*(The song finished,* ZETTA *takes a bow and exits. New sign: "Act 3: The Tower or The Tragedy of the Fall."* VERA *comes forward as the narrator. She beats a drum. A painted backdrop is lowered, showing a high, unfinished tower in a desert.)*

VERA. So long ago the stars were not yet cold
There was a land all desert, parched and dry
The people there were clever, we are told
And longed to look their dread god in the eye
And ask him why they were condemned to dwell
In such a desperate land, so hard and hot
That nothing was to choose 'tween it and hell
They loved their god, but feared he loved them not
And so in grief and anger did they bake
A thousand thousand bricks of straw and mud

Forgetting what befell the lord's own snake
When he presumed to know more than he…shud
    But as they built their tower high and wide
    It pleased them so, their rage turned into pride

> (ZETTA *in costume as the Builder, and* DOG *as the* WORKER,
> *come on.*)

ZETTA / BUILDER. Stupendous! Magnificent! The tallest thing in existence! You know, Worker, when I look at what we've done, I marvel. It must be the greatest wonder of the universe.

DOG / WORKER. If you say so.

ZETTA / BUILDER. A brilliant achievement: a tower to trump the heavens!

DOG / WORKER. I'd rather stay on the ground.

ZETTA / BUILDER. What are you complaining about? You'll be paid for your labor.

DOG / WORKER. That's what I'm afraid of.

ZETTA / BUILDER. Shut up and get back to work. We want to finish this level by nightfall. There are some who say that soon we'll be high enough to look God in the eye and demand some answers. About time!

DOG / WORKER. I'll work, but if any God-teasing goes on, I'm out of here.

> (VERA *makes a scary thunder-effect with her drum, and they stop
> and look up.*)

ZETTA & DOG. Uh oh.

VERA. The tower rose, and waked their sleeping god
Who raged to see how high they'd dared to go
He'd made them to be meek and tread the sod
And so he sent down plagues to bring them low

> (DOG *and* ZETTA *cower as* JO-JO *enters in costume as the
> Plagues. She runs around them, shrieking horribly—and then
> stops short, having run downstage and come face-to-face with the*

Scavengers. The Scavengers stand, raising their weapons. There's a moment of dead silence.)

DOG. *(Belatedly:)* Bark! BARK BARK BARK.

COKE. Be-still thy fucking dog or I'll be-fucking-still him for good.

ZETTA. Dog. C'mere, Dog.

COKE. Know thou all, it is thy glory to be the prize of the great, the grasping, the rapacious Coke, scavenger of scavengers.

BUD. And me. Bud the scavenger. Fuck yeah.

COKE. My eyes are keen, my feet tireless, and my hands loose not their grip for fuck-all. What-ere I see, that do I possess, and re-possess. I can wring usefulness from the very stones, from the very air if I choose! Be thou all assured, you will be well used, and never wasted. Pack all that was thine, now mine, that we may return in triumph.

VERA. A moment, if I may speak. Can it have escaped your notice that we are vaudevillians? Surely you must respect the sacred protected status of the traveling player.

ZETTA. That's right, there, lord scavenger. Only ignorant old savages don't know better nor that.

BUD. Fuck. Yeh. What I fucking said, Coke.

COKE. *(To* BUD:*)* Thou useless fuck, be fucking still. *(To* VERA:*)* We know about vaudevillians. But our Wendy is dead and recycled, praise her usefulness.

BUD. Praise it.

COKE. And the next one yet to be found. See? Betwixt and between and all bets off. Thou'rt raw material to me, nothing more. *(To* ZETTA:*)* Insult me again and I'll lay thee open like a gutted fish. Pack it up.

(He has spoken. The Vaudevillians slowly turn to obey. But:)

BUD. Well, but, fuck. What about the play?

COKE. What?

BUD. What about the rest of the play? I would see it. I would see how it ends. Dost not thou want to see it? *(To the Vaudevillians:)* Play fucking on, or know the wrath of Bud!

ZETTA. You want to see the rest of the play, it your call and all, just slay the word.

COKE. Ah, fuck yeah. I would see it finished. Let the play proceed. But fuck with us and thou'rt dead fucked, dost hear?

> (ZETTA *bows slightly and draws the other Vaudevillians into a huddle.)*

ZETTA. *(Aside:)* Command performance, if ever. But an audience an audience, what-ever-all. Give me time to think, one thing. You all okay to go on?

VERA. Most assuredly. As you say, time to think. After all, anything can happen in the theater.

COKE. SHUT FUCKING UP AND ACT!

ZETTA. From the entrance of the plagues. When-ever-all you ready.

> *(They resume their places.* VERA *plays the thunder-effect,* ZETTA *and* DOG *cower.)*

VERA. And so he sent down plagues to bring them low.

> (JO-JO *runs in again as the Plagues, and circles* ZETTA *and* DOG *as* VERA *speaks, beating her drum before each plague.)*

VERA. The Plague Of What-You-Lookin-At's
The Plague Of Big Ideas
The Plague Of Flag-Waving Border-Raving Killer Toads
The Plague Of Rockem-Sockem Godheads
The Plague Of Sick Machines
The Plague Of Tiny Blood Bugs
The Plague Of Crashing Techno-Rocks From Space
The Plague Of Dinosauritis
The Plague Of Neighbor-Slaughter
The Plague Of Long-Distance Rains O' Terror

The Plague Of Accidental Armageddon
The Plague Of The New Darkness!

(ZETTA confronts JO-JO.)

ZETTA / BUILDER. Why do you torment us?

JO-JO / PLAGUES. You know why.

ZETTA / BUILDER. Why did he make us, if he was going to destroy us?

JO-JO / PLAGUES. It's your own pride that destroys you.

ZETTA / BUILDER. Why does he hate us?

JO-JO / PLAGUES. He loves you but you betray him.

ZETTA / BUILDER. He betrays *us!*

JO-JO / PLAGUES. You never know when to stop, do you? It's too late. Your day is done. Your tower will be shattered, your workers decimated and scattered into the desert, never to build again.

(She pulls a knife, raises it. DOG stares at it, moving closer.)

JO-JO / PLAGUES. And you, Builder, architect of defiance, you must now pay for your sins. You wanted to speak to God? Come and see him now!

(JO-JO goes to stab ZETTA. But DOG leaps between them and is stabbed. There is a moment of silence as DOG holds the knife in his chest, staring at JO-JO. Then he crumples to the ground and is still.)

ZETTA / BUILDER. *(Ad-libbing in confusion:)* Laborer, it is not your part to die.

(ZETTA kneels down and touches DOG. Breaking character:)

Dog? Hey, Dog?

Knife real. He dead.

(To JO-JO:)

That my death he took, meant for me. Why?

(JO-JO *doesn't answer.* ZETTA *looks at* VERA.)

Well? You the true hand on the hilt. How about some of your famous truth?

VERA. But of course. You have only to ask.

ZETTA. Why you want me dead?

VERA. The usual reason. For what you have that I want. All rather moot now of course, but trust Jo-Jo to stick to a plan regardless.

BUD. *(To* COKE:)This play fucking sucks.

COKE. *(To Vaudevillians:)* YOI! THIS PLAY FUCKING SUCKS!

VERA. Our heartfelt and profound apologies, gentle viewers. The play has come to an untimely end. Not to put too fine a point, one of the actors is dead.

COKE. What, truly dead? Dead in fact? Not playacting dead?

BUD. What the fuck?

VERA. Truly dead, dead in fact and not in fiction. Lamentably, yes.

BUD. *(To* JO-JO:) Thou overacting fuck-up! Why-fucking-for didst thou so?

COKE. The dog was our prize, not thine to sacrifice. Hadst cause? Speak!

(*All eyes are on* JO-JO. *After a scant hesitation, she begins to improvise.*)

JO-JO. Hadst cause? Hadst fucking cause? Listen thou fucks and thou shalt know that this dog, this dead dog, this dead fuck of a dead-fucked dog was the evilest, vilest, badest dog of all. He could not be trusted, no, not so far as fuck-all. No one was safe from this heinous marauding brute. He woulda ripped out thy throats as thou slept, brave scavengers, first chance, or tried, and win or lose we'd a been fucked. If fail, thou'd a figured we were in on it and kill us all. If he succeed no odds for us, he'd get us sooner or later too. It was a wicked blood-thirsty man-eating monstrous wicked cruel beast of a bad bad dog and I did us all a fucking favor.

(Slight pause. JO-JO and COKE have locked gazes.)

BUD. What a load of stinking fuck-all.

COKE. (To BUD:) Shut thy fucking hole.

BUD. It's a lying little fuck! Let's gut it and teach it a lesson.

COKE. Touch her and die slow and horrible. (To ZETTA and VERA, referring to DOG:) Pack up the meat, and make haste. We must return to make the feast before it spoils.

ZETTA. No.

BUD. Fuck, another fucking tribe heard from.

COKE. What false understanding of me gives you this foolish courage, prize?

ZETTA. No faux four-one-one, Coke, but something I know you don't. Kill me, you live and die an ignorant fuck.

(COKE seems prepared to risk this, but BUD holds his arm.)

BUD. Stay, stay, for fuck's sake. I would know what it thinks it knows.

COKE. Speak, before you die.

(ZETTA rises, taking her moment.)

ZETTA. Your Wendy dead, and you chasing through the wide world for what, such poor prizes as seedy old vaudsters and dead dogs? You see, but you blind. You hear, but you deaf. This-all's your lucky day, deserve it or not. What you most of all need be under your noses, inside your reach, here to bring you glory to the end of your days for being the ones to scrounge it. Still don't know what-all? I should let you go on plain old dumb-fug as you are, but for pity's sake I will speak and end all suspense. Your Wendy dead but she rise again, recycled and good as new, ready to guide you. Where she? You long to learn. I tell you: She here!

(She turns and unexpectedly indicates VERA. *General amazement, including from* VERA.*)*

Conceal yourself no longer, O Useful One. The moment for revelation be at hand. Tell what only the Wendyness of all Scavengers know. Expound the reason for the vaudevillian taboo, and so they will know you.

*(*VERA *and* ZETTA *regard each other.)*

Your moment be come, O Most Resourceful. Recycled soul of the Wendy joined with your own. Cast off your temporary guise of the Vera and speak free. The truth will save us all, the truth as only the Wendy know it.

(Slight pause.)

VERA. *(Decisively, to the Scavengers:)* I had intended to observe you yet a while longer in my disguise, to see for myself the state of my scavenger kingdom. This wretched player has revealed me precipitously, and yet perhaps the moment has indeed come. The soul of your late Wendy, Praise her Usefulness—

COKE & BUD. *(Automatically:)* Praise it. Wendy's Here To Stay.

VERA. —has been recycled and restored good as new in me. Great and wise are the two who have found me. You will have glory when we return. Your usefulness will be much admired and rewarded.

(The Scavengers hesitate.)

BUD. *(To* COKE:*)* Is't true, think you?

COKE. If be so, as may be, that you are our salvaged leader, tell us this. Why are vaudevillians taboo? It is something only the Recycled One can explain.

VERA. Did not your previous late Wendy ever elucidate this question for you?

COKE. She forbade, under pain of terrible retribution.

BUD. She never explained fuck-all.

VERA. And now you expect me to reveal what she in her wisdom left shrouded? You are treading on the hem of a great mystery. I will say this, my children, listen thou well. The vaudevillian is the repository of all that was and all that may be. She is the key. She is the translator of our souls. More than this, more than all, listen thou, dear scavengers: she is that rare and precious pearl lying in this dark, drear, perilous sea: she is *entertainment.*

Further than this I cannot nor I will not speak. Kill us all and be damned for ignorant outlaw barbarians. Or accept me as your Wendy, and let us return to scavenger territory where you will be feasted in triumph for your brilliant resourcefulness in having found me, where you will have the choice parts of every sacrifice and the intense and pliant admiration of anyone you fancy.

(The Scavengers exchange a pragmatic glance.)

COKE. Fuck yeah.

BUD. Fucking right.

COKE & BUD. *(A roar:)* FUUUUCK.

COKE. Right. Thou'rt her all right. Anyone doubt it, is fucked.

VERA. Splendid. Well, let us delay no longer. Come, Jo-Jo.

BUD. *(Referring to JO-JO:)* Tarry a fucking moment. What is it? Prize, scavenger or vaudevillian?

ZETTA. She's mine. She killed my dog. Leave her to me.

VERA. A sort of justice in that, I concede —

COKE. She's mine! I fucking caught her!

JO-JO. Fuck you! I'm not your fucking prize!

BUD. What the fuck art thou then?

COKE. My prize or my mate. Choose.

(Everyone else is dumbfounded. JO-JO considers the offer.)

JO-JO. If mate, keep my own weapons?

COKE. Fuck yeah.

VERA. Jo-Jo, if I may interject—

JO-JO. Fuck when *I* say, or thou'll feel my knife.

COKE. *(To* BUD:*)* Witness it.

BUD. Witnessed.

JO-JO. *(To* COKE:*)* Deal.

(COKE *tosses her one of the weapons. She brandishes it.)*

Fuck yeah!

JO-JO, COKE, & BUD. *(A celebratory roar:)* FUUUCK

VERA. Well. If the wedding's over, let us depart.

(JO-JO *strides off, the Scavengers following.* VERA *lingers a moment, looking at* ZETTA *on the ground by* DOG's *body.)*

VERA. You do have a gift for improvisation.

A happy ending, all things considered.

I never would have expected it of him.

Best of luck in China, my dear.

(She exits. Slight pause.)

ZETTA. Okay, Dog. They gone.

(DOG *comes back to life.)*

DOG. Close one.

ZETTA. Quick of you, playing dead and all like that.

(DOG *shrugs.)*

You thought that a real knife, didn't you? Hey?

DOG. No. I don't know. Yeah.

ZETTA. Damn-all, Dog, what kinda dumb-fug trick?

DOG. Vera told me — I thought —

ZETTA. I know. Jo-Jo spilled the cat while we setting up for rehearsal. I was going to take a dive, get Vera off guard.

DOG. You could have let me in on it.

ZETTA. Well, you not being all so comunicado your own self! What you get for being a stubborn old close-mouthed mutt.

DOG. It was complicated!

ZETTA. Yeah, yeah.

DOG. Dammit, Zetta!

ZETTA. Don't you dammit me! Man! Gonna have to keep you on a tighter leash, pulling dum-fug sacrificial tricks like that.

DOG. Never again, trust me!

ZETTA. Damn right!

(Another violent earth-wobble.)

ZETTA & DOG. WOOOOOOH!

(They fall down.)

DOG. Ow.

ZETTA. *(Re: the change of season:)* Hey. What you think?

DOG. Feels like spring.

ZETTA. It do, it surely do. About time.

DOG. You said we might get to the sea in the spring.

ZETTA. I did so say. And we close. Sans doubt, we could do it.

DOG. And then China?

ZETTA. Sure, Dog. China be next.

DOG. I might not be a dog anymore.

ZETTA. Oh. Yeah?

DOG. Yeah. I might. I might become, you know. Human.

ZETTA. Well, it your call.

DOG. I know.

ZETTA. It'd change things. You and me. Be different.

DOG. I know.

ZETTA. Might not be bad. Might not be bad what-all.

DOG. I'm going to think about it.

ZETTA. Okay. You let me know.

You want to stick around here day or two?

DOG. No. No, let's hit the road.

ZETTA. Pack it up, pup-man.

> *(They repack the cart as* ZETTA *plans:)*

We get to the sea, there be people to ask. Always people close to the sea, poor dumb-fugs. Ever now and again they get all swallowed up, but more come to take their place. That people for you. But so there'll be a town, we can give 'em a show, get ourselves directions how to head toward China.

> *(If they haven't finished the packing by now,* ZETTA *begins to quietly sing one of their songs and* DOG *joins in, singing as they work, casually, playfully, helping each other, enjoying the return to routine. Ready to go, they take a look around.)*

ZETTA. You okay, there?

DOG. Yeah. Yeah.

ZETTA. Come on, then.

> *(DOG in harness begins to pull the cart while playing, as* ZETTA *pushes, helping to guide the cart. They exit, singing in a walking rhythm:)*

ZETTA & DOG. *(Singing:)*
DON'T ASK ME WHY
DON'T ASK ME WHAT
DON'T ASK ME NOTHING NOTHING NOTHING NOTHING
    BUT
HOO HOO, HOO HAH
WE'RE WALKING
JUST WALKING
WALKING TO CHI-I-NA

End of Play

Walking to China

Liz Duffy Adams

2. The King of China
He sent to me
A messenger of such immense civility
Hoo hoo, hoo hey
Just walking
Yeah walking
Walking to Chi-i-na

3. No one know where
That China be
We only know it where the sun come out the sea
Hoo hoo, hoo hoh
We're walking
Just walking
Walking to Chi-i-na

The Wang-Tailed Wallow

Liz Duffy Adams

2. The Wallow and the Ju-jee caught the 84-snap
Say hey and a hey till you bust a stangle
Then the gazabo copped it up the hinky-hap
Ho, ho, the wrangle

3. The Jujee pulled a woolly on the 22-snout
Say hey and a hey till you bust a stangle
So the Wallow hollered sammy till they cheesed it out
Ho, ho, the wrangle

4. The limp-a-lone snooker snagged the Jujee's last bap
Say hey and a hey till you bust a stangle
But the bulls biffed Cokey so they tipped the tap
Ho, ho, the wrangle

Weed World

Liz Duffy Adams

I'm just a weed-y girl___ in this

weed - y seed-y world___ with not much left to do___ but sur -

vey the gloom-y view___ Of the end of what we knew___ So I'd

Bluesy, expressive

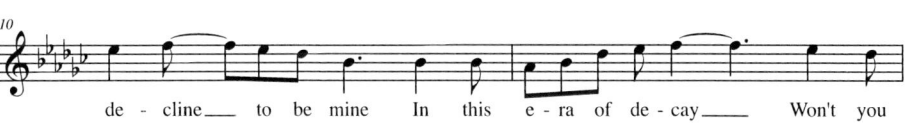

like to say___ to__ you... In this age of slow de-cline Don't you

de - cline___ to be mine In this e - ra of de - cay___ Won't you

say with me you'll stay___ And as a weed-y girl and boy___ What's left of

Human Blues

Liz Duffy Adams

Crit-ter in the bush-es, crit-ter in the sky — Don't know no-thing, they just live and they die — Crit-ter in the ri-ver, crit-ter in the sea — Don't know no-thing and they happ-i-er than me I know one thing, I know it chap-ter and verse How-ev-er bad it been, it gon-na keep get-ting worse I got the hu-man blues — O - o - o-oh the hu-man — blues —

2. The apple of Eden is a sour old fruit
Filled with bitter wisdom from the twig to the root
That apple it leave an evil taste in the mouth
Once it get in it ain't never get out
I know one thing, know it upside and down
When the water rise, everybody get drown
I got the human blues
O-o-o-oh the human blues

3. Know enough to mutter, know enough to moan
Know enough to know I can't never go home
Know enough to holler, know enough to howl
Know enough to know I know nothing at all
I know one thing, got it nailed to the floor
Although it do me no good, I always got to know more
I got the human blues
O-o-o-oh the human blues

Walking to China

Liz Duffy Adams

2. The King of China
He sent to me
A messenger of such immense civility
Hoo hoo, hoo hey
Just walking
Yeah walking
Walking to Chi-i-na

3. No one know where
That China be
We only know it where the sun come out the sea
Hoo hoo, hoo hoh
We're walking
Just walking
Walking to Chi-i-na